It is raining

Photography by John Pettitt

Dear Grandma,

It is raining here today.

Dear Grandma,
It is raining here today.

I went for a walk in the rain.
Mom came, too.

Dear Grandma,
It is raining here today.
I went for a walk in the rain.
Mom came, too.

I ran in the puddles.

I kicked the water.

Dear Grandma,
It is raining here today.
I went for a walk in the rain.
Mom came, too.
I ran in the puddles.
I kicked the water.

I looked up at the rain.
It went into my mouth.

Dear Grandma,
It is raining here today.
I went for a walk in the rain.
Mom came, too.
I ran in the puddles.
I kicked the water.
I looked up at the rain.
It went into my mouth.

Mom got a leaf
and she made a boat.

Dear Grandma,
It is raining here today.
I went for a walk in the rain.
Mom came, too.
I ran in the puddles.
I kicked the water.
I looked up at the rain.
It went into my mouth.
Mom got a leaf
and she made a boat.

I made a leaf boat, too.

Dear Grandma,
It is raining here today.
I went for a walk in the rain.
Mom came, too.
I ran in the puddles.
I kicked the water.
I looked up at the rain.
It went into my mouth.
Mom got a leaf
and she made a boat.
I made a leaf boat, too.

We went home.

Dear Grandma,
It is raining here today.
I went for a walk in the rain.
Mom came, too.
I ran in the puddles.
I kicked the water.
I looked up at the rain.
It went into my mouth.
Mom got a leaf
and she made a boat.
I made a leaf boat, too.
We went home.

Dear Grandma,
It is raining here today.
I went for a walk in the rain.
Mom came, too.
I ran in the puddles.
I kicked the water.
I looked up at the rain.
It went into my mouth.
Mom got a leaf
and she made a boat.
I made a leaf boat, too.
We went home.
Love,
Lee